THE COMPOSITE GUIDE

IN THIS SERIES

Auto Racing

Baseball

Basketball

Bodybuilding

Extreme Sports

Field Hockey

Figure Skating

Football

Golf

Gymnastics

Hockey

Lacrosse

Martial Arts

Soccer

Softball

Strongman Competition

Tennis

Track and Field

Volleyball

Wrestling

THE COMPOSITE GUIDE

to **BODYBUILDING**

MARY HUGHES

CHELSEA HOUSE PUBLISHERS

Philadelphia

Produced by Choptank Syndicate, Inc. and Chestnut Productions

Senior Editor: Norman L. Macht
Editor and Picture Researcher: Mary E. Hull
Design and Production: Lisa Hochstein
Cover Illustrator: Cliff Spohn

Project Editor: Jim McAvoy
Art Direction: Sara Davis
Cover Design: Keith Trego

First Printing

1 3 5 7 9 8 6 4 2

Library of Congress Cataloging-in-Publication Data

Hughes, Mary.
    The composite guide to bodybuilding / by Mary Hughes.
        p. cm.—(The composite guide)
    Includes bibliographical references and index.
    Summary: Surveys the history of bodybuilding and profiles some notable
participants in this sport.
    ISBN 0-7910-5861-1
    1. Bodybuilding—History—Juvenile literature. 2. Bodybuilders—History—Juvenile literature.
[1. Bodybuilding—History. 2. Bodybuilders.] I. Title: Bodybuilding. II. Title. III. Series.
GV546.5. H84 2000
646.7'5—dc21
                                                                00-022842

CONTENTS

CHAPTER 1
Lifting on the Lam   7

CHAPTER 2
Sculpting Bodies   13

CHAPTER 3
Iron Pumpers Who Primed the Pump   21

CHAPTER 4
Arnold, the Austrian Oak   29

CHAPTER 5
Redefining Muscle, Redefining a Sport   37

CHAPTER 6
Winning Over Women   45

CHAPTER 7
The Shape of Things to Come   51

Chronology   59

Glossary   60

Further Reading   62

Index   63

1
LIFTING ON THE LAM

In 1965 a young soldier was captured by the military police as he climbed over a wall at an Austrian army base. For his punishment, the enlisted man was jailed for seven days, sentenced to sleep on a cold stone bench with nothing but a single blanket to cover him. Very little food was brought to his tiny jail cell during the days he was imprisoned.

Although he was hungry and shivering from the cold, 18-year-old Arnold Schwarzenegger didn't complain. He was content, warmed by the memory of where he had been, what he had done, and what he had accomplished outside the walls of the army base. Arnold Schwarzenegger had not been caught trying to escape from camp. He was caught trying to climb back over the wall to return to boot camp. He had been AWOL (absent without leave); he had gone off the base without permission. For that, he was locked up in a solitary army prison cell upon his return to camp.

His capture by the Austrian military police was hardly significant compared to what Schwarzenegger himself had captured during his stolen hours of freedom: the attention—and the respect—of the bodybuilding world.

In Austria all young men must serve in the army for one year. Arnold Schwarzenegger had just begun serving his year in the military when he received an invitation to compete in a

Arnold Schwarzenegger, 1965 winner of the Mr. Europe Junior title, strikes a bodybuilding pose. Schwarzenegger's physique and charisma helped to transform the sport of bodybuilding in the late 20th century.

bodybuilding competition in Stuttgart, Germany, on October 30, 1965. Arnold wanted very much to compete, but he knew that the Austrian army would excuse him from camp only if there was a serious emergency, such as a death in his immediate family. There was no point in asking to be granted leave to enter a bodybuilding contest; his request would surely be turned down.

But Schwarzenegger could not just cast the invitation aside. He had spent the last five years of his life training for just such a competition, and he couldn't bear the thought of letting this opportunity slip away. He tossed and turned several nights, losing sleep as he decided what he should do, but ultimately he realized he could not lose sight of his goal. He was determined. He would deal with the consequences of going AWOL later. Right now, he had a dream to pursue and a goal to reach. He was going to become the greatest bodybuilder in the world, and he planned to get started by entering the contest in Stuttgart.

Once Schwarzenegger had made up his mind, there was no turning back. He crawled over the wall enclosing the army camp with only the clothes on his back and money for train fare. He couldn't afford first-class fare and was forced to travel from Austria to the competition with a third-class ticket on a train that stopped at each station. It took an entire day to reach Stuttgart.

During the long, exhausting train ride, Schwarzenegger tried to visualize the posing routine he would do for the judges at the contest. Never having been in a contest before, he had only the pictures of poses he'd seen in muscle magazines to go by. He idolized bodybuilder Reg Park, and had committed many of his poses to memory. Arnold's plan was to somehow string together several of his favorite poses to form a routine.

Arriving in Stuttgart tired, empty-handed, and a little nervous, Arnold had to get set for the contest. In his autobiography, *Arnold: The Education of a Bodybuilder*, Schwarzenegger remembered, "I had to borrow someone else's posing trunks, someone else's body oil."

He hoped he'd be able to get some tips on just how he should pose and perform by watching the competitors who took the stage before he was scheduled to go on, but he was disappointed with the routines he witnessed. They weren't any more sure of themselves than he was. To Arnold, they didn't seem very polished or professional, not at all like the posing pictures he'd seen of Reg Park in the muscle magazines, or the posters of Park that had covered the walls of his bedroom in his parents' home. He'd be better off remembering how Reg Park had looked and moved as the title character in his favorite movies in the *Hercules* series.

As it turned out, none of the performances he'd seen, nor the pictured poses he'd memorized, would figure greatly in his own premiere performance. When his turn came, his movements became purely instinctive. As Schwarzenegger recalled in *Arnold: The Education of a Bodybuilder*, ". . . the instant I stepped out before the judges, my mind went blank. Somehow I made it through the initial posing."

The judges who watched young Arnold Schwarzenegger pose on that Stuttgart stage were impressed. His muscular body gave testimony to his years of strenuous training, causing speculation as to the potential that this powerfully-built young man possessed. The judges asked that he return to the stage for what is called a "pose-off" among the top contenders. When the judges reached their decision, Arnold Schwarzenegger was declared Mr. Europe Junior 1965.

Arnold got an inkling, then and there, of what his life was to become. Happily, he now knew that he was destined for greatness in the sport that he loved. He vowed once more to become the greatest bodybuilder in the world. He envisioned what was in store for him: this was only the first of the titles and trophies he would amass.

Titles and trophies, unfortunately, don't necessarily afford winners their train fare, so the victorious Schwarzenegger borrowed some money and caught a bus back to boot camp. Caught as he was climbing back over the wall, Schwarzenegger relied on the wonderful memories of his triumphant trip to get him through the week he had to endure in solitary confinement. Seven days in the slammer weren't going to diminish in any way the fact that he was Mr. Europe Junior.

It wasn't long before word of Arnold's achievement reached high-ranking army officials. They were proud that one of their men had won such a prestigious award. Arnold was granted a two-day leave, and his work assignment was changed. He was commanded to work out in the gym for six hours a day, lifting weights. It wasn't a good idea to lift weights for six hours straight, but he was being watched by soldiers who would have him put in jail if he stopped his training. That was, after all, his new assignment. To the army's way of thinking, Schwarzenegger had been commanded to train, so he had better be training—at all times. Arnold quickly learned how to stretch out his weight-training routine so that it would last for six hours. Since the army had only barbells and weights, Arnold was glad that he had brought some dumbbells and several of his weight-lifting machines to boot camp. His extra equipment helped him to vary his routine and work more of his body's quickly developing muscles.

He was also allowed to eat as much food as he wanted in order to help bulk up his body. Army food isn't necessarily the best quality food in the world, but Arnold made do by eating huge quantities of it. In that way, he made sure he was getting enough protein from the poorer cuts of meat while burning off the excess calories. By eating five times a day, and pumping iron every afternoon, Arnold Schwarzenegger quickly built his weight up from 200 pounds to an impressive 225.

It was no longer just a dream. Arnold Schwarzenegger was on his way to becoming the best-known bodybuilder in the world. But more than that, he was turning a page in bodybuilding history, bringing the sport from its historic roots in Greek and Roman times into its current modern era. With his fun-loving personality, his determination and dedication to his sport, and the innovative techniques that he and his iron-pumping buddies would introduce to bodybuilding, Arnold Schwarzenegger was ready to revolutionize the age-old sport that he loved.

2 SCULPTING BODIES

The worlds of art and bodybuilding have been intertwined throughout history. As art imitates life, so does life imitate art. Bodybuilding was practiced in ancient Greece, Rome, and China, as evidenced by early artwork, which featured the well-toned, muscular bodies of athletic males. Sculptures and paintings from these civilizations often depicted athletes in action, such as an archer drawing back his bow, or two muscular opponents wrestling.

The word "athlete" comes from the the Greek word, "athlos," which means "a contest." Today's athletic contests sport a very long lineage back to Grecian feats of strength and derring-do, for it was ancient Greece that gave the world its very first Olympic Games in 776 B.C. Originating as a religious festival, the Games would take place every four years in Olympia, a fertile valley in Greece that was considered sacred. The tradition of holding the Games in Olympia continued for 1,000 years.

The early Olympic Games were no casual contests. Training for the athletes who were to compete in the Games was a full-time affair for the 10 months prior to the beginning of each Olympics. Competitors were scrutinized by the 10-member Olympic panel, who would judge each athlete according to not only their physical prowess in a contest but also the contestant's parentage, character, and physical endowments.

In the late 1800s, European-born body-builder/strongman Eugen Sandow traveled in vaudeville shows in the United States, amazing audiences by lifting 19 people and a dog on a board that rested on the back of his neck. In 1893 he appeared at the Chicago World's Fair, where he was touted as "the Strongest Man in the World."

Because women were not permitted to compete in those early games, it was the body of the male athlete that would often be represented in the art of this period. Greek and Roman sculpture dating back to the 4th and 5th centuries B.C. glorified the male body.

Art historian Eleanor C. Munro, in her *Encyclopedia of Art*, says of the Greeks, "When they began to make images of their gods, they gave them the most perfect human forms they could imagine and create, lithe and controlled as an athlete, as grave and contained as an Athenian girl."

According to Munro, at about 483 B.C., "After three centuries of experiment, Greek sculptors had mastered all points of human anatomy and proportion. Now they set out to create perfect forms."

Later, during the Renaissance, art would once again focus on the male body. In the late 1400s Italian artist Michelangelo Buonarroti journeyed to Rome to see the early work of the Greeks and Romans. He studied the statues that had remained intact, as well as those that had been reduced to ruins. He, too, wanted to achieve perfection in recreating the human form in his art. So desperately did Michelangelo want to understand the human body, perhaps nature's most complex and intricate mystery, that he forged a deal with Niccolo Bichiellini of the Santo Spirito Church, to receive permission to study the bodies of the dead. In exchange for the privilege of being able to closely examine corpses, Michelangelo fashioned a wooden crucifix for the prior and his church. Scrutinizing the bodies that he was permitted to examine, Michelangelo was able to better understand human anatomy, as he made countless sketches, or studies, of the cadavers. Unfortunately, being in such close contact with the bodies of the dead wreaked havoc on the young artist's health. Michelangelo had to abandon his morbid course of study several times in order to return to good health.

Michelangelo's marble sculpture *David* is one of the world's most cherished artistic masterpieces. Throughout time the statue has been described as heroic, precisely proportioned, athletic, courageous, and even as the perfect male. In many of his other works as well, Michelangelo presented to the world of art his vision of the perfectly sculpted male body. On the ceiling of the Sistine Chapel in the Vatican, Michelangelo painted his renditions of God and Adam as two perfectly chiseled, muscular male bodies, not at all unlike those of well-toned bodybuilders.

Just as the sculptors of ancient civilizations sought to carve perfection from marble, so, too, do bodybuilders seek to work and perfect their physiques by lifting weights. Bodybuilding began such a long time ago that much of its history is shrouded in legends. Bodybuilders themselves pass down the stories, trying to piece together the history of their sport.

Sig Klein began his own bodybuilding career in 1919. He related a long anecdotal history of the sport to Charles Gaines for the book *Pumping Iron: The Art and Sport of Bodybuilding.* Below is a much abridged, condensed version of his story:

Napoleon had defeated the Prussian army in 1806, but not the spirit of the Prussian

Michelangelo's sculpture David is a tribute to the artist's love of anatomy and classical Greek sculpture. It took Michelangelo three years to carve the statue out of a block of marble. Now located in the Galleria dell'Accademia in Florence, Italy, David is considered a symbol of strength and perfect human form.

people. Since Napoleon had forbidden Prussia from arming its men, Frederich Ludwig John attempted to come up with a viable alternative to weaponry. He popularized the idea of weight lifting in an attempt to improve the physical condition of the nation's men, so that they would be able to defend their country. As a result, small gymnastic clubs featuring modern weights became popular throughout Germany during the early 1800s.

During this time, strongman competitions were very popular in Europe. Felice Napoli of Naples was one of the more popular strongmen because of his superior showmanship. He impressed Louis Attila, born in 1844 in Baden-Baden, Germany, with his style and finesse. Attila studied under Napoli and soon became known as a premier performer in his own right. Attila performed his feats of strength before the royal family in England, receiving much praise for his strength and his showmanship.

As his reputation and fame spread, Attila set up a school in Brussels. An art student from Leyden University came to Attila for training and told him about a young model with an amazing physique who had posed for his art class. Attila often heard such stories, but he encouraged the art student to invite the model to the bodybuilding class. When Attila saw the model, he was so impressed with the young man's physique that he took him on as a student of bodybuilding.

After training this model, Frederick Wilhelm Mueller, for several years, Attila challenged another well-known strongman, Sampson, to compete against Mueller. The audience gasped at the model's magnificent muscles and beautiful body as he decisively defeated strongman Sampson in the challenge. Reportedly, the British began buying dumbbells and gymnasiums sprung up all over England after Mueller's exhibition of strength.

Frederick Wilhelm Mueller changed his name to Eugen Sandow, and then changed the focus of the typical strongman exhibitions in England. Instead of just proving his strength, the native of Prussia revealed to the public just why he had such power, showing off his muscled body. He wowed audiences by being a showman. Instead of simply lifting the standard weights in barbell form, Sandow impressed the crowd as he lifted 19 people and a dog on a board resting on his neck.

His crowd-pleasing antics caught the attention of American businessmen, who gave Sandow passage to America. But it was American showman Florenz Ziegfeld who came up with the proper vehicle to fully flaunt Sandow's sculpted form. Ziegfeld first show-cased the strongman in "Sandow's Trocadero Vaudevilles," a traveling show that toured major theaters in the United States.

Ziegfeld made Sandow the toast of Chicago's 1893 World's Fair, heralding him as "the Strongest Man in the World." Wanting fair-goers to be aware of the link binding body-builders to art, Ziegfeld carefully considered how he could best display Sandow's well-developed muscles. With white powder cover-ing his magnificent body, Sandow assumed the classic poses of Greek and Roman statues against a contrasting black velvet background. He looked like a living sculpture. Standing 5' 9" and weighing 180 pounds, Sandow had 18" biceps, 25" thighs, and a 49" chest.

In photographs remaining from that era, Sandow can be seen in various poses, wearing no more than a fig leaf and a pair of Roman sandals to further illustrate the connection between the art of the sculptor and the art of the bodybuilder. Sandow had indeed sculpted his own body into a shape comparable to one of Michelangelo's marble pieces.

After seeing Sandow in action, fitness-minded Americans began using dumbbells and haven't stopped since.

Sandow died in London in 1925. Today, the Mr. Olympia contest, one of bodybuilding's most important competitions, presents a bronze statue of Sandow to its winners.

IRON PUMPERS WHO PRIMED THE PUMP

3

The contestants for the "Handsomest Athlete in France" were judged in a way very similar to the first Olympic contests: muscularity, hair, eyes, teeth, and even the shape of their fingers and toes. In Germany, contests came down to issues of strength, period. Here in the United States, Al Treloar won Bobby McFadden's "Most Perfectly Developed Man in America" contest in 1903 at New York's Madison Square Garden, taking home $1,000 in prize money. Almost 20 years later, Angelo Siciliano won the title. Calling himself "Charles Atlas," Siciliano picked up the prize purse and brought in a little extra spare change by putting out a how-to manual that wound up being published in seven different languages, selling 70,000 copies annually.

Atlas called his bodybuilding manual a course in "Dynamic Tension." His advertisement featured a cartoon which showed the proverbial big bully kicking sand into the face of a skinny young man and his girlfriend. The skinny youth vows to get even with the bully, and sends away for help in the form of the 12-page booklet from Charles Atlas. Later, the youth is hardly recognizable with his new physique as he preens in front of his mirror, flexing his newly-formed muscles. The next time the bully confronts the young man on the beach, it is the bully who is defeated, and the new bodybuilder becomes a hero in the eyes of his girlfriend.

Charles Atlas holds four men in the air in this 1936 photo. Known as "the World's Most Perfectly Developed Man," Atlas became famous for his bodybuilding techniques and his mail-order courses in "dynamic tension," which were supposed to help even the puniest person achieve great muscles.

John Grimek holds the trophy he won at the 1940 weight lifting championship at Madison Square Garden in New York, where he was judged the "best developed and proportioned amateur athlete," earning him the title Mr. America. Grimek also won the title in 1941.

Beside the cartoon about the bully and the young man, stands a smiling Charles Atlas, flexing his muscles, sporting nothing more than a pair of leopard skin posing trunks, with a reminder of his title, "the World's Most Perfectly Developed Man."

Another pioneer bodybuilder, Bob Hoffman, began publishing his *Strength and*

Health magazine in 1932. By 1936 the magazine had a circulation of 51,333. Hoffman would later advertise heavily in the magazine to help sell the soybean-based high-protein products that he endorsed as the precursor to today's health foods.

Hoffman was a national champion weight lifter, and boasted that he was also "the World's Strongest Man," but since no one entered that contest in his weight classification, the honor is somewhat dubious. Much like the skinny youth in Charles Atlas's cartoon, Hoffman was a real featherweight growing up in Pittsburgh, Pennsylvania. At the age of 15 he weighed 150 pounds, not much for a boy standing 6' 3". Lifting weights helped him gain some weight and muscle.

After fighting in World War I, Hoffman set up shop in York, Pennsylvania, beginning with his York Oil Burner Company. He made sure that his company had an athletic club, and he expanded the line of products he manufactured to include barbells along with heating equipment. It wasn't long before he abandoned the heating business to concentrate all his efforts on his York Barbell Company.

Acting as sponsor, coach, and sometime competitor to a team of weight lifters, many of whom worked at a nearby iron foundry, Hoffman found a great deal of success. His team of weight lifters captured all six weight classifications at the U.S. championships one year. Hoffman served on the President's Council on Physical Fitness under three different presidents. Over the years, members of Hoffman's weight lifting club included such world and Olympic weight lifting champions as Bill Good,

Joe Miller, Tony Terlazzo, John Terpak, Stan Stanczyk, John Davids, Pete George, and Tommy Kno.

In December 1938 Johnny Hordine's "America's Finest Physique" contest took place at Gardner's Reducing Salon and Gymnasium in Schenectady, New York. There was no overall winner, but three different winners in each of three different height classes. The next year the contest allowed both professionals and amateurs to enter. Bert Goodrich, a profes-

Stan Stanczyk of the York, Pennsylvania, Barbell Club, was the AAU weight lifting champion and a veteran of the 1949 Mr. America contest, where he won the 181-pound class and set a new world record of 917 pounds lifted.

sional muscleman, was declared 1939's overall winner.

That same year, the American Athletic Union (AAU) officially sanctioned bodybuilding by creating the Mr. America contest. Roland Essmaker was the contest's first winner, followed by John Grimek, a graceful poser who has been called one of the best bodybuilders of all time.

John Grimek, a York Barbell employee, was a star member of Bob Hoffman's York Barbell weight lifting team. Together, Grimek and Hoffman dispelled a myth held by the medical profession, and by many coaches and trainers as well. At the time, many people believed that working out with weights caused an athlete to become muscle-bound, leading to a lack of flexibility. Hoffman staged a demonstration to show that this was not the case. According to York Barbell's company historian, Jan Dellinger, "Grimek, a handsome devil with a fantastic body, stood on a chair and flexed and the doctors all said he was muscle-bound. John then bent from the waist and touched his in-steps with his elbows." Hoffman had Grimek demonstrate in several other ways just how flexible he was to the doctors before asking them, "Can any of you gentlemen do that?" Grimek competed in the 1936 Olympics and was a two-time winner of the Mr. America contest, and the 1948 Mr. Universe.

Ever the entrepreneur, Hoffman opened the Weight Lifting Hall of Fame and Museum at his York store. In 1970 the International Weight Lifting Federation named Hoffman "the Father of World Weight Lifting." Bob Hoffman died in 1985 at the age of 86. Today the Weight Lifting

Ben Weider, chairman and cofounder of the International Federation of Bodybuilders, pushed to make bodybuilding a demonstration sport at the 2000 Olympics in Sydney, Australia.

Hall of Fame and Museum displays artifacts related to the history of bodybuilding and strongman competition. The Hall of Fame and Museum also hosts the York Barbell Strength Spectacular, a three-day event that includes a powerlifting championship, strongman contest, and weight lifting demonstrations.

In 1946 Joe and Ben Weider formed the International Federation of Bodybuilders (IFBB) to rival the older American Athletic Union. Originally from Montreal, Canada, the Weider brothers insisted that they wanted bodybuilding to take center stage, not play second fiddle to a weight lifting competition. Their IFBB physique contests have done much to promote the specialized sport of bodybuilding, and the contests boast participants from over 80 countries. Weider Enterprises produces several bodybuilding magazines, including *Muscle and Fitness*, *Shape*, *Men's Fitness*, and *Flex*. Joe and Ben Weider's company also makes barbells and food supplements with bodybuilding appeal.

Joe Weider figured prominently in the career of Arnold Schwarzenegger. He invited the Austrian to compete in the IFBB's Mr. Universe contest in Miami, Florida, and asked Arnold to train in America for a year, with the stipulation that Weider could use photographs of Schwarzenegger in his *Muscle Builder* magazine. It proved to be a win-win situation for both men.

Following Steve Stanko, winner of the first Mr. Universe title in 1947, Steve Reeves dominated the sport of bodybuilding, popularizing it even further when he finally left the competitive circuit to make Italian gladiator movies. Reeves, born on January 21, 1926, in Glasglow, Montana, was a California bodybuilder standing 6' 1" and weighing 213 pounds. His handsome face and muscular body made him a natural to play the role of Hercules.

Another bodybuilder, Reg Park, who hailed from South Africa, also won bodybuilding competitions and the role of Hercules in such films as *Hercules and the Vampire*. Together, the two Herculean actors, Reg Park and Steve Reeves, captured the attention of a young boy in Austria who was an avid film buff, just beginning to discover the sport of bodybuilding.

ARNOLD, THE AUSTRIAN OAK

Arnold Schwarzenegger was born on July 30, 1947. He grew up in the tiny village of Thal in Austria. His mother, Aurelia, worked hard keeping the family's home clean. There was no running water and no refrigerator. Mrs. Schwarzenegger set out daily, walking from farm to farm, shopping for fresh food to prepare for her family. Like most other families living in post-World War II Europe, the Schwarzeneggers considered meat a luxury and only saw it on the dinner table about once a week.

Arnold's father, Gustav, was the chief of police, and the Schwarzeneggers lived in a house that had been built by the nation's royalty. By royal decree, both the chief of police and the area's forest ranger were to occupy the 300-year-old house, which meant the Schwarzeneggers lived upstairs, while the ranger lived downstairs.

Arnold and his brother, Meinhard, who was a year older than Arnold, were very active children. In his book, *Arnold's Fitness for Kids Ages 11–14*, Arnold describes what life was like for the Schwarzenegger boys. "There was always plenty of physical work around our house. From the time we were very young, Meinhard and I had numerous chores—splitting and stacking wood, carrying coal for the stove, cleaning the stove and oven of ash, and carrying water to the house from our well. But we also managed to

Bodybuilder-turned-actor Arnold Schwarzenegger poses at the German premiere of his 1999 film End of Days. *Schwarzenegger has starred in numerous successful films, including the* Terminator *movies,* Kindergarten Cop, *and* Total Recall, *in which his muscular physique has played a prominent role.*

find time for play and sports. Both Meinhard and I participated in gymnastics, soccer, and running and jumping contests in school. Our lives outside of school were just as active. We had neighborhood championships in badminton and volleyball, sledding on the hills in the winter, and swimming in the lake near our house and hiking in the mountains in the summer."

Mr. Schwarzenegger encouraged his sons to be competitive, often pitting them against each other in athletic contests. Meinhard was older and stronger and usually won. Arnold learned at a very young age that he did not like to lose. He vowed that someday he would be the very best in the world at something—even though he did not yet know what that something would be.

By the time he was 13, Arnold had discovered something else about himself. He wanted to be singled out and recognized when he did something well, so he began gradually moving away from team sports such as soccer and volleyball, and he gravitated to individual sports such as boxing, swimming, and throwing the javelin and the shot put.

Weight training was something that Arnold's soccer coach suggested for his soccer players. Arnold obliged and headed to the gym to do some weight lifting to help develop the leg muscles so important for soccer. He had no idea how pivotal that trip to the gym would become in shaping the course of his life. Later, he described the feelings that overcame him in his book *Arnold: The Education of a Bodybuilder* by saying, "I still remember that first visit to the bodybuilding gym. I had never seen anyone lifting weights before. Those guys were huge and brutal. I found myself walking around them, staring at muscles I couldn't even name, muscles I'd never even seen before. The weight lifters shone with sweat; they were powerful looking, Herculean. And there it was before me—my life, the answer I'd been seeking. It clicked. It was something I suddenly just seemed to reach out and find, as if I'd been crossing a suspended bridge and finally stepped off onto solid ground."

The regulars at the gym tried to warn him that he'd be sore, but Arnold honestly didn't think his young, athletic body was going to react badly to its initiation into the strenuous workout of the bodybuilder. Exhilarated by that first session, Arnold left the gym feeling great. It wasn't until he fell off his bike on his way home, unable to grip the handle bars with his hands, that he realized he might have overdone it. The next morning, he couldn't raise his arms to comb his hair and spilled the entire cup of coffee his mother set before him, which prompted his parents to voice their concern—for the first of many times—about his newfound obsession with bodybuilding.

Learning by trial and error, Arnold set out to be the best. He let nothing deter him, and found ingenious ways to practice both at the gym, which was an eight-mile bike ride away, and at home. While his body was developing, Arnold also developed a philosophy that would help to guarantee a successful future. "The secret," he said later, "is contained in a three-part formula I learned in the gym: self-confidence, a positive mental attitude, and honest hard work. Many people are aware of these principles, but very few can put them into practice."

Arnold began his required one year of Austrian military service in 1965. In the midst of boot camp he pulled off his AWOL escapade, making his way to Stuttgart to win his first bodybuilding competition, Mr. Europe Junior. From there, Arnold moved on to Munich in order to prepare himself for the Mr. Universe contest. He rented a room in an apartment where he shared a bathroom and had kitchen privileges. For income, he managed a health club, with every spare moment devoted to his own training. Every morning he worked out for two hours, focusing on his arms and shoulders. Every evening he worked out for two more hours, this time focusing on his legs, chest and abdominals. He gained an additional five pounds and felt ready for the competition.

Arnold's English was very limited. He flew to London, reciting the phrase, "I would like to go to the Royal Hotel, please," over and over during his first airplane ride. Unfortunately for Arnold, the phrase brought him to the wrong Royal Hotel, where some kindhearted travellers from Munich were able to ask for directions to the correct hotel, translate them for Arnold, and send him off in a taxi to London's other Royal Hotel, the one that was hosting the Mr. Universe contest.

His reputation had arrived at the Royal Hotel before him. Everyone wanted to see the young Austrian with the big arms. From the time Arnold's cab pulled up, he was mobbed. He had to abandon his notion of being able to blend into the background and just observe

When he began his body-building career, Arnold Schwarzenegger quickly realized that a tan helps to show off the veins beneath the skin, as demonstrated by this bodybuilder, who was voted "most muscular" at the Mr. Wisconsin contest held at the Wisconsin State Fair.

what such a big competition was like. He found himself at center stage. Looking back, Arnold admitted that he had not gone to the Mr. Universe contest seriously expecting to win but that once he got there and his self-confidence began to build with the admiration of other bodybuilders, he began to entertain the idea that he just might have a chance at the title. Then he caught sight of Chet Yorton, the tanned, polished American favorite. Arnold knew immediately that he was not yet ready to defeat Chet Yorton. He was right. When the judges' votes were tabulated, it was Yorton first, Schwarzenegger second.

Yet, even in defeat, Arnold learned a lot. He realized he would never again allow himself to enter a contest without mentally expecting to win. He now understood how a tan could help to make a bodybuilder's veins appear more prominently beneath the skin. When veins are not visible, it is because there is a layer of fat between the skin and the muscles. He saw what his weak points were and vowed to improve them through hard work, so that in the future he could become Mr. Universe.

One of the judges from the Mr. Universe contest, Wag Bennett, introduced Arnold to the finer points of showmanship and posing for contests. He convinced a reluctant Arnold to utilize classical music, rich with texture and depth, in his posing routines. It wasn't long before Arnold realized how much of an impact music could make on a routine. Soon he was taking a copy of the soundtrack to the film *Exodus* with him all over Europe whenever he performed for exhibitions.

Arnold also received help from his idol, Reg Park. After getting over the initial excitement of meeting his hero, Arnold was able to calm down and take in every word that Park shared with him. Naturally, the two bodybuilders talked incessantly about their sport, but Schwarzenegger noticed something else: He had become somewhat of a bully, always out to prove to everyone how big, strong, and masculine he was. He was constantly driving too fast, picking fights for no reason, getting into trouble with the police, and showing off to impress people—especially women. Reg Park wasn't like that. He didn't go around trying to prove himself but instead was content in knowing who he was. Arnold took heed, learned a valuable lesson in life, and became a better person for it.

Always striving to improve himself, Arnold Schwarzenegger made a conscious decision to avoid becoming overly muscle-bound by lifting too many heavy weights. He wanted to steer clear of a physique that looked massive. Like Reg Park, he strove to develop a showman's body, which would appear nice and muscular when he was standing relaxed and dramatically different when his muscles were flexed.

By observing, learning, and listening, the young Schwarzenegger made sure to note details that would enhance his chances of winning and to steer clear of anything that could harm them. He didn't let foreign cultures or languages stand in his way. Instead, he picked up new languages and customs each time he stepped over a border for a new competition. His patience, practice, and perseverance paid off. Arnold would dominate the sport for a decade, from 1965 through 1975, then capitalize on his celebrity by becoming a major motion picture star in the United States.

REDEFINING MUSCLE, REDEFINING A SPORT

5

Oddly, for a sport that has existed for centuries, bodybuilding did not achieve prominence in modern day athletics until the 1970s. Arnold Schwarzenegger, who would eventually be known as "the Terminator," may also be credited as somewhat of an "Originator." Arnold and his contemporaries managed to pull all the components of the time-honored sport together, giving it a new sense of unity. The muscles of the human body have remained as they were in the days of Michelangelo, but the equipment used to hone them has improved dramatically. New routines, techniques, and approaches to bodybuilding have eliminated much wasted energy and time. Knowledge of nutrition and diet have led the way to healthier athletes, who can now zero in on achieving the desired results that will help them win trophies and titles. Music and choreography have become an integral part of prejudging and posing.

A plethora of products compete for the bodybuilder's attention at health and fitness stores. Which oil will work best to maximize an athlete's best features on exhibition day? What vitamins will help him build the endurance he needs to pursue his goals? As the competitive event draws near, what final preparations must a competitor make? How can dehydration be avoided while the athlete tries to eliminate any excess fluids from the body? Even the latest

Bodybuilder Frank Zane, who beat out Arnold Schwarzenegger for the 1968 Mr. Universe title, is a three-time Mr. Universe and the coauthor of a fitness manual called The Zane Way to a Beautiful Body.

findings regarding ultraviolet rays and sun-screens have helped modern bodybuilders achieve the requisite tan with a minimum of sunburn.

Schwarzenegger did his best to bring body-building to the masses. After Arnold, the sport survives, enjoying perhaps more popularity than ever, since today's titlists benefit from his publicity. Today's bodybuilders have learned to market themselves and make themselves accessible to the media. Some contemporary

Though Lou Ferrigno, left, known for his role as the Incredible Hulk, had bigger measurements than Arnold Schwarzenegger, he lost to him in the 1974 and 1975 Mr. Olympia contests. In bodybuilding, size is less important than form and finish.

Arnold Schwarzenegger poses at the 1968 Mr. Universe competition in Florida, where he took second place.

contenders include Ronnie Coleman, Flex Wheeler, Lee Labrada, Lee Priest, Darren Charles, and Milos Sarcev. Few bodybuilders can make a living solely through their sport; many of them increase their incomes by selling books and products related to bodybuilding.

Arnold Schwarzenegger has coauthored several books, including *Arnold: The Education of a Bodybuilder*, written with Douglas Kent Hall, plus the original and revised editions of his *Encyclopedia of Modern Bodybuilding*, both of which he authored with Bill Dobbins.

Schwarzenegger has also produced a series of fitness books for children with author Charles Gaines.

Frank Zane and his wife Christine shared the writing duties in creating their manual, *The Zane Way to a Beautiful Body*. Christine Zane is the winner of multiple beauty contests. Frank Zane defeated Arnold Schwarzenegger in the 1968 Mr. Universe competition and captured that title again in 1970 and '72. He has also garnered first place titles in the Mr. World, Mr. America, and Mr. Olympia contests.

Thanks to the willingness of the world's most accomplished bodybuilders to share their secrets with eager readers, today's beginning bodybuilders can avoid some of the pitfalls and problems that once plagued the sport.

Bodybuilding has its own unique vocabulary. The "pump" is what the bodybuilder is after. It is the sudden sensation of having blood rush into a particular muscle after an exercise. *In Pumping Iron: The Art and Sport of Bodybuilding*, coauthor Charles Gaines writes, "A pump also makes you feel giddy and happy in the head." For the bodybuilder, "feeling pumped" or "pumped up" is what it's all about.

Before beginning a weight training program, athletes should start off with freehand exercises. These include push-ups, bent-leg sit-ups, bent-leg raises, deep knee bends, and chin-ups. Schwarzenegger suggests that freehand exercises be followed with a swim, a run, or a jog to avoid becoming muscle-bound.

Once the athlete has progressed with the freehand exercises, it is time to move into the gym. Concentrating on working large groups of

First, bodybuilders perform compulsory poses for judges, then they are allowed time to do freestyle poses. These bodybuilders emphasize their chest and shoulder muscles, top, then turn around to display their biceps, bottom.

muscles, these exercises include the bench press, the military press, barbell curls, leg curls, wrist curls, squats, and sit-ups.

After a workout utilizing those exercises, the body will understandably be sore. For that reason, bodybuilders rest the body. The period after a workout is called the recovery period. During that period, muscles that were worked are given a chance to rest. Bodybuilders also swear by plenty of sleep, along with some serious stretching to promote flexibility.

It may sound counterproductive, but a bodybuilder actually tears down a muscle in order to build it up. In order for a muscle to become bigger, the bodybuilder must rest that muscle after it is exercised. This allows the tissue that grows back to become slightly larger than it was before. That is why routines are staggered and vary from day to day to allow muscles their all-important rest.

Bulking up exercises help the bodybuilder get bigger, acquiring more mass, while exercises that are said to chisel down help to reduce specific areas of the body, carving and separating muscles from one another, giving each muscle better definition.

Graceful, sleek, polished muscles that appear natural and not forced give a bodybuilder finish. This quality escapes many bodybuilders and keeps them from capturing the top awards in competition. Lou Ferrigno, who catapulted to fame as the Incredible Hulk in the popular television series costarring the late Bill Bixby, actually had bigger measurements than Arnold Schwarzenegger, but as far as the judges were concerned, Ferrigno didn't have finish. Schwarzenegger did. In 1974 and again in 1975, Ferrigno lost to Schwarzenegger in the Mr. Olympia contests for that very reason. But Ferrigno's sheer size makes him a force to be reckoned with in the sport of bodybuilding. At 6' 6", weighing 275 pounds, "the Incredible Hulk" is indeed incredible. He's massive. Ferrigno later won Mr. Universe and Mr. America titles.

Each time a bodybuilder performs a particular exercise it is called a "rep" or repetition. A group of reps forms a set. For example, a bodybuilder might perform three sets of eight reps each of an exercise as part of his daily workout.

For the advanced bodybuilder, supersets combine sets of exercises, working muscle groups that naturally tend to work together. For example, the bodybuilder would go directly from working out one muscle or muscle group, such as the hamstrings, or backs of the thighs, to the quadriceps, or fronts of the thighs, without pausing. This requires very high energy on the part of the bodybuilder, but it helps to create a nice flow between the different muscles, which will now work together instead of independently.

Supersets help to balance out the body, making sure that muscles that naturally oppose each other are given an equal workout. For every muscle in the body there is an opposing muscle. The hamstrings and quadriceps in the legs are opposing muscles; in the arms, it is the biceps and triceps that oppose each other. The biceps are the muscles in the front of the arm that Popeye the Sailor Man liked to flex, while the triceps are located on the back of the arm.

Perhaps more important than either the set or the superset is the mind-set of the bodybuilder. Having a positive mental attitude helps the bodybuilder to visualize what he or she wants to accomplish and to have the personal strength to continue and realize that goal. Arnold Schwarzenegger proved again and again to himself, to the judges, and to the fans of bodybuilding that a healthy dose of confidence and conviction helps tremendously in competition.

6   WINNING OVER WOMEN

In 1980, the first Ms. Olympia contest took place in Philadelphia, Pennsylvania. Sponsored by the Association, a new group of bodybuilders including Arnold Schwarzenegger, Franco Columbu, George Snyder, and Bill Drake, the event was well-planned and well-received. Years of knowledge and experience, plus a knack for effective marketing, made for a smooth mixing of business and competition.

The women the world saw at the first Ms. Olympia contest were not the raw competitors that their early male counterparts had been. Arnold Schwarzenegger had laughed in disbelief when he was first approached for an interview and wound up asking more questions than he answered. In contrast, these women were polished, fit, and ready for the onslaught of interviews and constant coverage of the events.

By combining the competition with a convention that showcased dietary supplements, training equipment, and fashions that helped to enhance the body, the Association scored a major win. In a sense, they validated the sport for the new female competitors, armed as they were with the knowledge that bodybuilding for women needed to be presented to the public in a way that would minimize the number of people who were disgusted and maximize those who would recognize the health and fitness benefits of the sport.

More women started pumping iron in the 1980s, when the success of the first Ms. Olympia contest helped establish numerous women's bodybuilding championships. Shown is Ms. Olympia winner Rachel McLish.

Rachel McLish, winner of the 1980 and 1982 Ms. Olympia contests, parlayed her bodybuilding success into a career in the fitness industry, writing about weight training and conditioning. She also became an accomplished martial arts instructor.

Two of the seminars that were given during that weekend were very well attended: Arnold Schwarzenegger's "The Psychology of Bodybuilding," and Franco Columbu's "Strength and Injuries."

That first Ms. Olympia contest had 25 entrants. Those who finished in the top five were to be awarded trips to Venezuela. In all, the prize money totaled $10,000. Before a panel of four men and three women judges, each contestant had to participate in three rounds of competition. First, entrants were judged in a relaxed pose from the front, the back, and from each side. Next, contestants demonstrated six compulsory poses. In round three, each woman was given creative freedom to perform one minute of poses of her own choosing.

When it was all said and done, the top five winners were, in order: Rachel McLish, Auby Paulick, Lynn Conkwright, Corrine Machado, and Stacey Bentley.

Georgia Fudge, Carla Dunlop, Patsy Chapman, Cammy Lusko, and Suzy Green, all of whom competed at that first Ms. Olympia,

To maximize the benefits of weight training, body-builders perform sets of exercises intended to work on different areas of the body.

were some of the other pioneer women pumpers who helped to make that event a success. Just as the 1977 film *Pumping Iron* had broken new ground for men's bodybuilding, its 1985 sequel, *Pumping Iron II: The Women*, showcased the women of the rapidly growing sport.

Among the female bodybuilders, Joyce Vedral, Rachel McLish, Anja Langer, and DeBarra Mayo have pumped out books related to the sport to supplement their incomes and to help get beginners off to a good start. Shelley Beattie did her part to bring bodybuilding to the attention of the public by becoming an American Gladiator. Her husband, John Romano, was the culinary advisor for Gold's Gym in Venice Beach, California. He created a cookbook, *Muscle Meals*, designed to help bodybuilders of both sexes eat a well-balanced diet.

Joyce Vedral, who proudly shows off a physique that got better with age, wrote another cookbook for anyone wanting to incorporate the bodybuilder's way of eating into a weight loss program. Entitled *Eat to Trim: Get It Off and Keep It Off*, her cookbook features over 200 recipes, plus some photographs of her looking rather dowdy in her 20s and sensational at the age of 55.

Vedral's cookbook is a belated companion book to her 1993 volume on getting in shape called *Bottoms Up!* In it she thanks "Joe and Betty Weider for inventing and promoting the training principles used in this book and by the champions, and for (their) wonderful magazines: *Muscle and Fitness*, *Shape*, *Men's Fitness*, and *Flex*."

In her books, Vedral advocates that body-builders "break training" for one day each week, eating whatever they choose. This is the same strategy suggested by bodybuilding author Rachel McLish, who wrote *Perfect Parts* in partnership with Vedral. McLish and Vedral provide readers with two sets of workout regimes. One is designed for readers who wish to work out at home, and the other is for those who want to work out at a gym. Each regime is divided into nine segments intended to work out the different areas of the body. Exercises are clearly grouped to develop a specific area such as the chest, back, shoulders, biceps, triceps, abdominal muscles, buttocks and hips, thighs, or calves.

Anja Langer, a German beauty who has amassed many international bodybuilding titles, is the coauthor of *Body Flex-Body Magic* with Bill Reynolds. She offers her own personal bodybuilding regime, along with tips on nutrition and diet.

All of these books by women in bodybuilding help the female bodybuilder to see clearly how routines are modified for women and how women who pump iron can look their best.

THE SHAPE OF THINGS TO COME

As popular as bodybuilding may be, not everyone wants to develop bulging biceps. There are those who just want to improve their overall appearance and level of fitness.

Denise Austin is a physical fitness expert who advocates reshaping the body without bulking up. A gymnast since her childhood, Denise has made physical fitness a way of life. With her long-running televised exercise programs, first on ESPN and later airing on the Lifetime television network, Austin has been in the public eye for over 20 years, advocating physical fitness.

Austin's television viewers have witnessed her own body's transformation over time as she gradually incorporated weight training into her exercise routines. In the February 1999 issue of *Muscle and Fitness* magazine, Denise was prominently featured in a segment entitled "Girl Power." During an interview with Michelle Basta Boubian for the story, Denise admitted to deliberately changing her workout to acquire her newly toned physique through weight training. Austin said, "I've reshaped, firmed up, and leaned down. I've changed my look."

Always an advocate of moderation, Denise doesn't lift heavy weights. Moderate weights better suit her purpose, which is to sculpt the body, as opposed to building the body. Since she isn't out to create bulging muscles, she varies her routine to include every part of her body

While bulging biceps are the goal of many bodybuilders, fitness experts recommend that would-be bodybuilders exercise and get into shape before starting a weight lifting routine.

Arnold Schwarzenegger, center, stands with the winners of the Arnold Schwarzenegger Classic held in Columbus, Ohio, on March 2, 1996.

instead of focusing on the power movements of the bodybuilder. She also avoids the bodybuilder's high-calorie, high-protein diet, choosing instead to keep her calorie intake moderate and to eat a well-balanced diet. Like bodybuilders, she does drink lots of water every day. And, just as the bodybuilder zeroes in on specific muscles to strengthen and build, Denise targets specific body parts to tone and shape with her routine, which varies from day to day. Typically exercising six days a week, Denise divides her days into three spent weight training and three spent elevating her heartbeat with cardiovascular (aerobic) work-outs. It's a schedule that suits her lifestyle and her total sense of well-being.

As Denise Austin told *Muscle and Fitness* readers, "I believe it's important to enjoy life, and it's easier to do that when you feel good, and exercise makes you feel good. If you exercise regularly, you can keep a step ahead of the aging process. And weight training is the best way to fight the aging process." Echoing the sentiments of Arnold Schwarzenegger, Denise added, "Attitude is important. If you have a positive attitude, it shows in your face and your body."

Overall physical fitness is something both Denise Austin and Arnold Schwarzenegger advocate for today's youth. Each has been involved with the President's Council on Physical Fitness. Both athletes began their physical fitness training at an early age. Austin was competing internationally in gymnastics by the age of 12. And had Schwarzenegger not spent his childhood running, jumping, and actively participating in sports, it is doubtful that he would have won the title of Mr. Europe Junior at the age of 18. Before he even lifted his first barbell, or first touched a dumbbell, Arnold was physically fit, strong, and healthy.

Ellington Darden, Ph.D., is the author of several popular bodybuilding books. Aware that many of his readers are under the age of 18, he realizes that there are dangers facing young bodybuilders. In his *High-Intensity Home Training* manual, Darden spells out precautions for anyone under the age of 20 who wants to begin weight lifting. He advises that young bodybuilders follow the guidelines set by the

American Academy of Pediatrics, the American Orthopedic Society for Sports Medicine, and the American College of Sports Medicine.

These medical organizations are not opposed to weight lifting by teenagers, but they have very real concerns about youngsters lifting too much too soon. This is due to the nature of the growth process of the human body, which involves the epiphysis, or growth plate. Before a person reaches his or her final height, each of the long bones of the body are connected to a bone shaft by a growth plate, which is a wide band of cartilage. In normal bone growth, Darden explains, "bone cells gradually develop from the shaft. They start displacing the cartilage cells by turning into hard, new bone cells. The cartilage cells are then forced to move toward the ends of the long bones. As the cartilage moves outward, the long bones grow."

A pediatrician can tell by examining the growth plates whether or not a child has finished growing. If a child's growth plates have not yet closed, the child will most likely experience several normal growth spurts until he or she reaches their eventual adult height. Darden explains that until the growth plates have hardened, or "ossified" into bones, there is the potential to damage the growth plates by excessively heavy exercise.

So it is with good reason that experts recommend that the young weight lifter avoid Olympic weight lifting such as the clean and jerk or snatch. They also advise against powerlifting at an early age, which means teenagers should stay away from squats, bench presses, and dead lifts. Darden also advises young competitors to "avoid trying to see how much they can lift in a one-time, all-out effort."

This does not mean that the teenaged athlete must abandon weight training altogether. Darden and the organizations mentioned earlier suggest that training for those under the age of 20 should be done with lighter weights. A particular weight should be deemed too heavy for its lifter if he or she cannot comfortably perform eight to 12 repetitions using it.

Darden also recommends that teenage bodybuilders get a good night's sleep and plenty of rest. He suggests 10 hours of shut-eye each night for teens, with a 15-minute nap in the afternoon.

The art and sport of bodybuilding has blossomed into a multi-million dollar industry with worldwide interest and coverage. The advent of VCRs and cable television allowed both the curious and the aspiring bodybuilder access to a sport that was once holed up in sweaty gymnasiums and garages. No longer do those who are interested in bodybuilding have to venture to live competitions to catch a glimpse of the sport they love. Today, fans can enjoy a variety of monthly muscle and fitness magazines at bookstores and newsstands, surf through endless Internet sites dedicated to the sport, or catch a competition or exhibition on television. And, of course, with the increased popularity of bodybuilding—among both men and women—it's easier than ever to witness first-hand what the commotion is all about.

As is the case with beginning any new course of physical exercise, anyone wanting to begin a bodybuilding regime should first

Colombia's Maria Perea competes during the clean and jerk portion of the women's weight lifting tournament at the 1999 Pan American Games in Winnipeg, Canada. Children and teenagers should avoid weight lifting events like the clean and jerk or the snatch, as these exercises put a lot of stress on the body and can damage a young person's growth plates.

consult a physician and undergo a complete physical. An examination by a doctor could reveal conditions that might cause problems for an individual involved in strenuous exercise.

Once given the go-ahead by a doctor, the beginning bodybuilder should compare how-to magazines and manuals for the sport, and decide which regime best suits his or her purposes. From there it is a personal matter of mixing and matching up exercise routines, weight training regimens, dietary plans, the desired level of fitness, and the willingness to commit to a program.

Naturally, it helps enormously to get pumped up mentally about undertaking the bodybuilding challenge before attempting to get pumped up physically.

CHRONOLOGY

776 B.C.	The first Olympics are held in Greece.
500-400 B.C.	Greek and Roman artwork glorifies the body of the male athlete.
1400s A.D.	The Renaissance again has art focusing on the perfect male body; Michelangelo creates his marble masterpiece, *David*.
1800s	Frederich Ludwig John endorses weight lifting for the Prussian Army; gyms spring up all over Germany.
1844	Louis Attila of Baden-Baden, Germany, is born and later performs before royalty and sets up a school in Brussels for bodybuilding.
1893	Eugen Sandow, heralded as "the Strongest Man on Earth," is the toast of the World's Fair in Chicago.
1903	Al Treolar wins "the Most Perfectly Developed Man in America" contest at Madison Square Garden; nearly 20 years later, Angelo Siciliano changes his name to Charles Atlas and wins the same contest.
1932	Bob Hoffman begins publishing *Strength and Health* magazine.
1939	Bert Goodrich, a professional muscleman, wins "America's Finest Physique" contest; Roland Essmaker becomes the first "Mr. America," in a contest sponsored by the American Athletic Union.
1940	John Grimek is the second Mr. America and proves to members of the medical community that bodybuilders are not necessarily muscle-bound or inflexible.
1946	Joe and Ben Weider form the International Federation of Bodybuilders (IFBB).
1947	Steve Stanko becomes the first Mr. Universe; Steve Reeves and Reg Park dominate the sport and later become successful movie stars.
1965	Arnold Schwarzenegger goes AWOL from boot camp in Austria to travel to Stuttgart, Germany, to become Mr. Europe Junior. He will dominate the sport for years to come, then follow his idols Reeves and Park into a career in motion pictures.
	Frank Zane's bodybuilding career begins the same year that Schwarzenegger's does, but he outlasts "the Austrian Oak" by three years in competition.
1980	The first Ms. Olympia contest is held in Philadelphia and won by Rachel McLish.
1999	Ronnie Coleman wins the IFBB's Professional World Cup.

GLOSSARY

BARBELL refers to a metal bar with added weight. A barbell may have permanently fixed weights at either end, or it may have changeable plates, held in place by what is called a collar. To balance the barbell, plates of equal value are placed at each end. A barbell is meant to be held with both hands.

BICEPS are the muscles on the front of the upper arm. There is also a muscle in the leg, just below the hamstrings, which is referred to as the Biceps Femoris.

BUILDING UP is the process of having a muscle get bigger. It cannot occur unless a bodybuilder actually tears down that muscle, and then allows it a period of rest, usually 48 hours, before exerting it again. This allows the tissue which grows back to become slightly larger than it was before.

BULKING UP exercises help the bodybuilder get bigger, acquiring more mass.

CHISEL DOWN refers to the process in which a bodybuilder reduces specific areas of the body, carving and separating muscles from one another, giving each muscle better definition.

DEFINITION describes a muscle that has very little fat surrounding it. When a muscle is well developed and not hidden by fat, it is said to be clearly defined.

DELTOID refers to the muscle in the back of the shoulder.

DUMBBELL refers to a metal bar which is meant to be held in one hand. Like a barbell, a dumbbell may have permanently fixed weights on either end, or it may have changeable weights.

EXERCISE in bodybuilding is a particular movement targeting a specific muscle, with the express purpose of causing that muscle to strengthen and grow.

FLEX means to contract a muscle. Flexing a muscle makes the fibers of that muscle shorten as the muscle is squeezed.

FREEHAND EXERCISES are exercises done without weights, such as push-ups, bent-leg raises, deep knee bends, and chin-ups. These are generally done before beginning a weight training program to help an athlete get in shape for the rigorous work ahead.

FREE WEIGHTS can be used anywhere, because they are not attached to the gym floor. Both dumbbells and barbells are free weights because of their portability.

HAMSTRINGS are the large muscles on the back of the thighs.

LATS is short for latissimus dorsi. Located in the upper back, on either side of the spine, these are the muscles that unmistakably identify a bodybuilder. Well-developed lats cause the elbows of a bodybuilder to jut out further than the shoulders, because they naturally lift the arms up and away from the body.

PUMPED OR PUMPED UP has become synonymous with being excited about something, but it has its roots in bodybuilding. A bodybuilder is naturally excited to see that progress is being made as a result of all the lifting and exercising. During a strenuous workout, muscle tissue becomes temporarily enlarged because of increased blood flow to a particular area. Experiencing a pump can make the bodybuilder feel giddy.

PUMPING IRON is a phrase credited to Johnny Gunn of Birmingham, Alabama. Reportedly, Gunn first used the expression in the late 1950s, to mean lifting weights.

QUADS OR QUADRICEPS are the large front thigh muscles. They are opposed or balanced by the hamstrings, the muscles on the back of the thighs.

RECOVERY PERIOD is the time given to a muscle group to rest. Typically, a bodybuilder will work on major muscle groups on one day and minor muscle groups on the next.

REP OR REPETITION refers to one complete exercise. After completing one rep, the body is back in the same position it was to begin the exercise, ready to repeat it again.

RESISTANCE stresses out a muscle so that it can develop. The heavier a weight, the more resistance.

REST is a calculated, timed pause between exercises or sets of exercises. A rest allows a muscle to recuperate and recover enough strength before it is required to repeat another exercise or set. Rests range from zero to 60 seconds. Keep in mind that an entire muscle group may rest while another group is being worked, so that the bodybuilder can minimize the overall time of the workout. To avoid confusion, the long rest period between daily workouts is usually referred to as the recovery period (see above).

ROUTINE refers to the entire group of exercises targeted for any one body area. For example, a bodybuilder is finished working his biceps for the day when he has completed his biceps routine.

SET defines how many times an exercise is performed. There are a specific number of reps in a set and a specific number of sets in a routine. Supersets combine sets of exercises, working muscle groups that naturally tend to work together.

STRETCH is the opposite of flex. Stretching a muscle lengthens the fibers of that muscle.

TEARING DOWN a muscle is the first step in having that muscle become bigger and stronger. After a muscle is torn down by the bodybuilder, it is allowed to rest, usually for 48 hours, before it is exercised again.

WEIGHT has to do with the heaviness or resistance of a weight used in a particular exercise. The heavier the weight, the more resistance.

FURTHER READING

Darden, Ellington. *High-Intensity Home Training*. New York: Putnam, 1993.

Doherty, Craig A. and Katherine M. *Arnold Schwarzenegger: Larger Than Life*. New York: Walker Publishing Company, 1993.

Gaines, Charles and George Butler. *Pumping Iron: The Art and Sport of Bodybuilding*. New York: Simon & Schuster, 1974.

Langer, Anja and Bill Reynolds. *Body Flex-Body Magic*. Chicago: Contemporary Books, 1992.

Lipsyte, Robert. *Arnold Schwarzenegger: Hercules in America*. New York: Harper Collins, 1993.

McLish, Rachel and Joyce Vedral. *Perfect Parts*. New York: Warner Books, 1987.

Schwarzenegger, Arnold and Douglas Kent Hall. *Arnold: The Education of a Bodybuilder*. New York: Simon & Schuster, 1977.

Schwarzenegger, Arnold and Charles Gaines. *Arnold's Fitness for Kids Ages 11-14*. New York: Doubleday, 1993.

Schwarzenegger, Arnold and Bill Dobbins. *The Encyclopedia of Modern Bodybuilding*. New York: Simon & Schuster, 1985.

Vedral, Joyce L. *Bottoms Up!* New York: Warner Books, 1993.

Vedral, Joyce L. *Eat to Trim*. New York: Warner Books, 1997.

Zane, Frank and Christine Zane. *The Zane Way to a Beautiful Body Through Weight Training for Men and Women*. New York: Simon & Schuster, 1979.

INDEX

American Athletic Union, 25, 26

Atlas, Charles, 21–22

Austin, Denise, 51–53

Beattie, Shelley, 48

Bennett, Wag, 34

Bentley, Stacey, 47

Chapman, Patsy, 47

Charles, Darren, 39

Coleman, Ronnie, 39

Columbu, Franco, 45, 46

Conkwright, Lynn, 47

Darden, Ellington, 53–55

David, 15

Davids, John, 24

Drake, Bill, 45

Dunlop, Carla, 47

Essmaker, Roland, 25

exercises, 40–43, 54–57

Ferrigno, Lou, 42

Fudge, Georgia, 47

George, Pete, 24

Good, Bill, 23

Goodrich, Bert, 24–25

Green, Suzy, 47

Grimek, John, 25

Hoffman, Bob, 22–24, 25

International Federation
  of Bodybuilders, 26, 27

Klein, Sig, 15

Kno, Tommy, 24

Labrada, Lee, 39

Langer, Anja, 48, 49

Lusko, Cammy, 47

Machado, Corrine, 47

Mayo, DeBarra, 48

McLish, Rachel, 47, 48, 49

Michelangelo, 14–15, 19, 37

Miller, Joe, 24

Olympic Games, 13–14, 21

Park, Reg, 9, 27, 34–35

Paulick, Auby, 47

Priest, Lee, 39

Reeves, Steve, 27

Sandow, Eugen, 17–19

Sarcev, Milos, 39

Schwarzenegger, Arnold, 7–11,
  27, 29–35, 37, 38, 39–40, 42,
  43, 45, 46, 53

Snyder, George, 45

Stanczyk, Stan, 24

Stanko, Steve, 27

Terlazzo, Tony, 24

Terpak, John, 24

Treloar, Al, 21

Vedral, Joyce, 48–49

Weider, Ben, 26, 27

Weider, Joe, 26, 27, 48

Weight Lifting Hall of Fame
  and Museum, 25–26

Wheeler, Flex, 39

York Barbell Company, 23, 25, 26

Yorton, Chet, 33

Zane, Christine, 40

Zane, Frank, 40

Ziegfeld, Florenz, 18

MARY HUGHES graduated from the University of Maryland with a degree in Radio, Television, and Film. She enjoyed substitute teaching for many years before tackling her current assignment as a computer lab tech at an elementary school in Maryland. Her first book, a biography of comedian Jim Carrey, written for Chelsea House Publishers, was named to the New York Public Library's list of "Best Books for the Teen Age" in 1999. An avid baseball fan, Ms. Hughes writes feature articles about ballplayers in the Baltimore Orioles organization. Writing as she does about both the minor and major leaguers, she often gets an inside peek at just what it takes to make it to the big leagues and how special it can be to remain there. Her favorite ballplayer is her teenage son, Mark Hudson.